# The Brilliant Concept and Design of the USA

Vic Biorseth

A Product of

www.CatholicAmericanThinker.com

ISBN:1541387767
ISBN-13:9781541387768

# DEDICATION

To the reeducation of those Americans who have been misinformed about their own American heritage. This is dedicated to the undoing of decades of malicious disinformation, indoctrination and propaganda masquerading as formal education and news reporting. Formal education in America should, at this moment in history, be recognized as driven from above by an anti-American *Ministry of Indoctrination*. Established Mainstream News Media, both printed and broadcast, should be recognized as driven from above by a *Ministry of Propaganda*. This has come to be because Political Parties, which are unconstitutional entities not mentioned in the Constitution, have assumed all government power, over and above the Constitution's three branches of legitimate government. The Parties have become the "Establishment" that runs the nation, with ever changing political agendas, and will little or no attention to the Constitution.

This is my attempt to at least shine a light on that, and reveal to the misinformed some small part of the beauty and the  inspiration that is behind the concept and design of the USA.

My previous book, *Culture = Religion + Politics*, goes into more detail.

# ACKNOWLEDGMENTS

I must here acknowledge my wife Marcie, for her patience during all my long hours banking away at a computer keyboard when I should have been doing other things around the house.  And my nephew Mark, for all the times I didn't have time for him, because I was consumed by the incessant need to write, and to publish on my website things that always seemed more important than whatever else was going on.

This booklet represents one webpage on that website, which may be found on the internet at

http://www.CatholicAmericanThinker.com/Inspired-Brilliant-Republic.html

It seemed to me that some might want a cheap, simple hard copy to give to children or grandchildren or others to "wake them up" to what they now have, and to what they stand to lose if they are inattentive to American Politics.  This is presented so that those not on-line or not into the internet can find the truth about their own nation's original design and intent.

So many Americans today do not know about the original design of the Senate, which was to avoid what we see today, which is Senators who have become mere professional politicians.  Too many today do not know the original purpose and critical importance of the Electoral College, which is under attack and is now at risk, the same as the Senate.

Most of this is born of a simple love of history and a perhaps too large personal library, and love of certain historical characters, George Washington in particular.  And now, with the development of the internet to the point it has developed today, the availability of an on-line "library" that I  could never afford.  Information is available today, electronically, that might have taken years and years  to research, back as little as thirty ears ago.  My website is

wwwCatholicAmericanThinker.com

In the website, this webpage is loaded down with links to other webpages and other sources backing up what is said here.  Go to the website for verification of source material.

## Opposition to Tyranny of Man, or Tyranny of Government.

For entirely too many generations now evil men have been polluting the minds of children through anti-American education, anti-American "News" reporting and a distinct lack of honest education in America's history, her Declaration of Independence and her Constitution. What has been lost, on multiple generations now, is an honest recognition of the unique and beautiful nature of the nation they were born in. It is a government organization unlike any other in all of world history, and millions of American citizens are blind to it, if not opposed to it.

Untold millions of Americans have been miss-lead into anti-Americanism.

Most of the rest of my website is dedicated to explaining and undoing that damage, and identifying the treachery behind it; here we will try to provide a quick and simple refresher-course in what America is all about, for those who have been misinformed, mal-educated, indoctrinated and propagandized by the domestic enemies of the Constitution, right here among us, now infecting all levels of American society. Some of them are evil conspirators and would-be tyrants, some of them are "organized" *agent provocateurs*, some of them are *convinced* in their purposely malformed minds, but all of them are American domestic enemies, nonetheless, having been trained into blind, unreasoned hatred of America.

What America's First Patriots were waking up to before the Revolution was the tyranny of monarchy. Under hereditary monarchy, government was only "good" government, from the people's point of view, when the reigning monarch was a "good" monarch. Whenever he was a tyrant, however, then the people were essentially his slaves, to do with as he pleased.

The tyranny of King George, and the insufferable tyranny of his governors and his established government in the Colonies is precisely what the Revolutionary War was fought over. Once it was won, the winners were loath to establish anything similar. They were adamantly opposed, in their majority, to rule by one man, and to rule by any form of government of men who were not in some way accountable to someone other than themselves for their governing actions.

The government had to be at least accountable to but not subservient to the people being governed. How to strike that balance between accountability to the people and yet still governing the people was the problem they wrestled with.

## Opposition to Democracy as Tyranny of Majorities.

They knew that Democracy as a form of government was impossible, and was a form of tyranny of majority doomed to failure in its very design. Examples of pure Democracy might be:

- A lynch mob. Let's vote on whether my opponent should be hanged or not. Everyone in favor say aye; the ayes have it; get the rope.
- The Predominant Political Party Rules; Let's vote on whether this smaller Party must yield all of its food to us, so that we eat more and they eat less, or not at all.
- A national or international organized labor union, or a union of unions. Let's vote on whether all employers everywhere should pay us all $100 per hour for whatever work we do or don't do, or we strike and shut down whole industries and even nations until they do.
- Two wolves and a sheep voting on a dinner menu.

Democracy as a system can only work in small groups deciding small matters. A club, or a civic group, etc., small enough to sit in deliberation around a conference table. Even then some system such as *Robert's Rules of Order* are needed just to keep things civilized, or the meeting will break down into chaos, with the most dominant personalities controlling the whole discourse.

Democracy is doomed to economic failure by its very nature. A democratically elected government will soon learn how to bribe voters with the voters own money, collected in taxes. And citizens will soon learn to vote in politicians that promise them more "benefits" or "welfare" from the government, feeding the inclination to work less and depend on government more for their own subsistence.

Enter the corrupt politician, promising a chicken in every pot, pretending interest only in "the good of the people". And he will always get his votes, for the people are capable of being corrupted, too.

Since only free citizens produce wealth, and since governments can only collect and spend wealth, eventually a declining citizen's production of wealth will starve the ever increasing government citizen benefit and welfare budget, the system will fail, and the whole nation fall into economic ruin.

So they recognized Democracy as an impractical, very foolish and always eventually very corrupting form of government. The political temptation to satisfy personal self interest over the better interest of the whole nation is too great to always be resisted. Officers of the government soon become professional politicians rather than honest statesmen.

And, of course, even a tyranny of the majority remains a tyranny.

## Sovereignty of States within the United States.

Another problem America's First Patriots wrestled with was the existing sovereignty of each existing Colony. Once out from British rule, would they be able to retain their own distinct Colonial governments, or would each be swallowed up into a larger new nation, in which they would have no distinct Colonial voices?

Each Colony was born of Colonists who came here, at least partially, in order to escape the various denominational religiously oppressive governments in British and European nations. There, the monarch was the head of the state Church, and all were required to tithe the state Church, and forbidden to believe, worship or practice religion in any other denomination, by force of law.

That was the sort of religious tyranny they originally came here to escape.

To protect themselves from being coerced to follow a denomination not of their choosing, the original Colonists each established their own official state denomination in their Colonial Charters or Constitutions. They would have no one dictate their religion to them. The Denominations were:

| | |
|---|---|
| Rhode Island | Baptist |
| Pennsylvania | Quaker |
| Maryland | Roman Catholic |
| Connecticut | Congregational |
| Georgia | Church of England |
| Massachusetts | Congregational |
| North Carolina | Church of England |

| | |
|---|---|
| New Hampshire | Congregational |
| South Carolina | Church of England |
| Virginia | Church of England |
| Florida | Catholic (Spanish era) Church of England (British era) |
| West Indies | Church of England |
| New York | Church of England |
| Delaware | Undifferentiated Christian |
| New Jersey | Undifferentiated Protestant |

Thus we see that Catholicism along with all of the predominant American Protestant Denominations, collectively, formed what came to be known during the Revolutionary era as America's "General Christianity".

Each Colony was loath to allow anyone outside the Colony to ever override their own Colonial laws, especially those pertaining to their already established Catholic or Protestant Denominational worship and practice in the living of their lives. Many were opposed to a federal government being superimposed above them for this reason alone.

Some preferred a simple military alliance of the Colonies for mutual defense, modeled after the *Iroquois League*, an alliance of different tribes of Indians in which the allied tribes all agreed that an attack on one was an attack on all, and all would unite in war against the attacker. That way they could each maintain their own unique Colonial ways of life as separate governmental entities.

## The Concept, and the Declaration.

So the problems the First Patriots faced in forming a new nation were legion.

- Some of the Colonies - not all - wanted to always remain independent sovereign entities.
- None of them would ever accept any higher level of government imposing any form of religion over their own legally established Colonial religions in their own Colonies.
- Almost none of them would ever accept monarchy, *ever again*.
- And they knew that Democracy was a corrupting and eventually impossible form of government, for it was doomed to eventual failure in its very concept.

The failure of the first attempt at *Colonial Communist Government* was then fresher in Colonial memory than it is today. The first Colony of the Pilgrims, under William Bradford, had attempted a version of "Communism" until it proved so unworkable that most of them were dying of starvation. Then, as a last ditch survival effort, they unleashed individual citizen *Liberty* and *Private Property*, and the prospering of America began, with a loud *Free Market, Capitalistic Roar*, which was soon heard by the whole world.

Where the First Patriots, who were all Representatives of their various Colonies, differed the most in their religion was in their diverse *Theological Doctrines*, stemming from the *Love Of God* Commandments that they all recognized in different ways. And what they all held most in common was in their *Moral Doctrines*, stemming from the *Love Of Neighbor* Commandments, which they all held in very nearly total agreement. These were the social and societal rules that formed the backbone of Western Civilization, and could be thought of as "civilizing" rules of conduct. There, they were in agreement.

Even those among them who had fallen prey to "Enlightened" thinking and "Modern" theories, and who had fallen into atheism, agnosticism, or who dabbled in the then popular intellectual fad of Deism, agreed with the high civilizing morality of Christianity. And they had all been raised in Christian households under strict Christian rules and education, whatever they might have become later. So all were imbued with a Christian sense of morality and decency from birth.

In those days, even atheists could quote Scripture, for the most commonly read book was the Bible. It was the most common tool for the teaching of English to children in the home. And even the most devout atheists still recognized the *wisdom* to be found in the Bible.

In finding a way to "declare" their new revolutionary nation and its purpose, the First Patriots concentrated on what they held most in common - the Moral Commandments, and Christian Morality. How to synthesize it all, in a manner acceptable to all, without making it specifically "Catholic" or favoring any Protestant Denomination led to increasing emphasis on Natural Law, and collective agreement on the Divine Author of Nature. And on Objective Truth. For, after all,

God's Law = Natural Law = Truth = *Objective Reality*.

## Applied human reason soundly defeats the pure materialist argument.

Objective Truth exists that is untouchable and unchangeable by man. It is totally independent of man. What man thinks is *subjective*; what God makes is *objective*. No matter what any man or any men think bout it or try to do about it, it remains Objective Truth, immutable and true for all time. It's a simple matter of reality. We can discover it; we can study it; but we cannot ever change it.

Men can only falsely describe it or deny it. No one can change it.

So, with recognition of Natural Law as a tool, and Justice as a goal, the First Patriots began to come up with the idea, or ideology, upon which to base their new nation. The intent was to develop a government that could never become tyrannical and that would provide Just government - meaning *justice for all citizens*. A tall order.

And what, exactly, was "Justice" under the Natural Law, and how could it be equally applied by government to all citizens?

Justice, in the moral order, seeks the *Common Good* for the whole citizenry, so that they may be secure and safe, so that they may *prosper*, and so that the whole population may *flourish*.

## **The Natural Law Rights.**

The opening paragraph of the Declaration of Independence speaks of the Colonies breaking with England, "to assume among the powers of the earth, the separate and equal station to which the Laws of Nature and of Nature's God entitle them" and forming a new nation.

The second paragraph spells out the basis of *American Justice*, upon which the new nation would be built.

> We hold these truths to be self-evident, that all men are created Equal, that they are endowed by their Creator with certain unalienable Rights, that among these are Life, Liberty and the Pursuit of Happiness.

The recognition and safeguarding of these rights were held to be the necessary means to establish Justice in the new nation.

1. "Equality" meant, at its essence, the right to be heard; the right to *present your case*. It means equality before the law. It means equal access to the seats of justice, equal rights, equal liabilities, equal responsibilities, equal liberty, and equal opportunities. Combined with Liberty, it means you are perfectly free to work to improve your own condition, any moral and legal way you can. In good justice, no man may be denied this right without due process of just law.

2. "Life" meant, at its essence, that Human Life is sacred, assumed innocent, and to be protected by law from its natural beginning until its natural end. That all living human beings have an absolute legal right to continue to live. In good justice, no man may be deprived of this right without due process of just law.

3. "Liberty" meant, at its essence, that a man is free to move about without restriction, to take up residence wherever he chooses, to educate himself in whatever interests him, to apply himself in whatever enterprise or work he chooses, so long as he and he alone chooses to do it. In good justice, no man may be deprived of this right without due process of just law.

4. "Pursuit of Happiness" meant, at its essence, the right to honestly work to improve one's own condition. To "get ahead". To earn, and to save, and to build. In a nutshell, it is the right to acquire, possess, accumulate and trade in *Private Property*, in any form: currency; land; livestock; crops; timber; minerals; inventions; art; buildings; technology - in fact, any legitimate thing man can imagine. In good justice, no man may be deprived of this right without due process of just law.

These civil rights were declared to be "unalienable", established by God, and not subject to be modified or taken away by any man or by any government. They were *permanent*. They were *Natural Law Rights*. No mere man, and no mere government established by man, had any right or true ability to take them away from the citizenry. Despite what anyone might do to suppress these rights, they would always exist, as a matter of being part of *Objective Reality*.

## The Purpose For Being.

The second paragraph of the Declaration continued, establishing the new nation's very purpose for being:

— That to secure these rights, Governments are instituted among Men, deriving their just powers from the consent of the governed, — That whenever any Form of Government becomes destructive of these ends, it is the Right of the People to alter or to abolish it, and to institute new Government, laying its foundation on such principles and organizing its powers in such form, as to them shall seem most likely to effect their Safety and Happiness.

After all, what good is the governmental establishment of true *Justice*, if after establishment, Justice may simply be taken away, and the people have nothing to say about it?

The Election Process is the tool by which the citizenry may altar government that becomes unjust and fails in protecting the civil rights of the citizenry.

When the Election Process itself is corrupted or fails to restore Justice to the citizenry, it is the right of the citizenry to abolish the government entirely and start over. This has never happened in America. *Yet.* The right remains.

## **The Constitution.**

"... to secure these rights, Governments are instituted among Men, deriving their just powers from the consent of the governed ..."

"... to institute new government, laying its foundation on such principles and organizing its powers in such form, as to them shall seem most likely to effect their Safety and Happiness."

Based on these Declared Principles, the Authors framed and developed the Constitution of the USA. The Constitution lays out the entire organization of our government, supplies its complete operating instructions, the Bill Of Rights and later Amendments further cement the rights of the citizens and the rights of the still sovereign states.

All of the citizen rights laid out in the Constitution, the Bill Of Rights and the Amendments are related to and stem from the Declaration's Natural Law Rights, of Equality, Life, Liberty and Property. And all four of these Natural Law Rights are firmly established among all the others as absolute Constitutional Rights.

Life, Liberty and Property are explicitly laid out in Amendment V of the Bill Of Rights. Equality is conspicuously absent there, due to the unsettled argument for the continuation of slavery put forth by the Planters representing North Carolina and Georgia, who threatened to walk out and end the USA before it was born.

Thus, in order to get ratification and become a nation, we see the ridiculous "three fifths" of a human being compromise clause in Section 2 of Article I. And thus, we see the infamous *escaped slave* clause in Section 2 of Article IV.

These Southern Planters would form the Democrat Party, which would become the Secessionist Party, which would become the Confederate States of America, which would lose the Civil War, and which would then give birth to the KKK, which passed the infamous Jim Crow laws, and which would oppose the MLK equal justice movement, and which ultimately became the Marxocrat Party we see today.

The tricky Marxist Party of the Obamunists and the Clintonistas, of Globalism vs Sovereignty, of Open Borders, anti-Capitalism, Socialist Redistribution, wild environmental fraud as a political tool, and the Party of purposely organized social chaos and disorder.

Whether they liked it or not, they lost the Civil War, Amendment XIV finally solidly established the American civil right to Equality for all citizens, and the "three fifths" clause and the "escaped slave" clause were taken out by Amendments XIII and XIV.

Justice won.

The purpose for the Constitutional government is laid out in the Preamble of the Constitution, as follows:

> **We the People** of the United States, in Order to form a more perfect Union, establish Justice, insure domestic Tranquility, provide for the common defence, promote the general Welfare, and secure the Blessings of Liberty to ourselves and our Posterity, do ordain and establish this Constitution for the United States of America.

Article I establishes the Congress, made up of a House of Representatives and a Senate; all laws must originate in Congress, which holds sole Constitutional authority to legislate law.

# The House of Representatives.

The House is the most numerous body of the two; there is one Representative to represent every 30,000 citizens in each State. The Representatives are the only elected federal officials who are elected by pure popular vote. States are generally divided into districts or precincts by population, so that each US Representative is elected by and represents one distinct State district of approximately 30,00 citizens. Each such district in each state elects its own US Representative. Thus, the Members of the House of Representatives are (in the original design) the only pure Democratically elected officers in the entire Federal Government. Each Representative has one vote.

Numbers of State Representatives to the US Congress change with population changes, kept track of by national census taken on a ten year cycle. States are "redistricted" to keep numbers of Representatives in sync with populations. Citizens are free to move from district to district and from state to state at their own pleasure.

# The Senate.

Originally, the Senate was comprised of two Senators from each State, *chosen by the Legislature thereof,* for six Years; and each Senator has one Vote.

The ingenious purpose of this arrangement of State Legislatures selecting their own US Senators was to safeguard State Sovereignty, and prevent a purely Democratic election from allowing highly populated States from overwhelming lower populated states with sheer numbers. If and when that happened, the States would no longer be Sovereign.

No law can pass without passing both Houses of Congress. The House represents the citizenry, but the Senate represents the States. Senators serve at the discretion of the duly elected State Governments who sent them to Washington and who keep them there for six years, or so long as they are satisfied with their performance.

Woodrow Wilson, a Marxist of the *Progressive* persuasion, managed to pass two Amendments to the detriment of the Republic, and in the interest of transforming America into a Democracy, which would eventually implode into Socialism, economic collapse and then tyranny.

Amendment XVI allowed a graduated income tax, in agreement with the Communist Manifesto and allowing elected officials to begin to bribe the voters with the people's own money.

Amendment XVII transformed the Senate into a pure Democratically elected body, no different than the House of Representatives, except that the two Senators ran state-wide political campaigns, because they "represented" the whole state's population. And *Not* the state's duly elected government. Now, the whole Congress is Democratically elected, and, *Legislatively*, we are no longer a Republic, as originally designed. Law is now legislated as in a Democracy.

High population centers can now overwhelm lower populated states with pure popular vote counts, the very thing the Framers intended to prevent by keeping the Senate out of politics altogether. Senators today are mere professional politicians, rather than Statesmen.

The Congress now represents only the citizenry, not the States.

We have long recommended repeal of Amendment XVI and repeal of Amendment XVII. America can only survive and prosper as a Constitutional Republic. Not as a Constitutional Democracy.

Prior to President Wilson's major Progressive victory in passage of Amendment XVII America's main, and almost sole source of revenue was from tariffs on imported goods for sale, and certain excise taxes. The authorization is found in the first paragraph of Article I Section 8, as follows:

> **Section. 8.** The Congress shall have Power To lay and collect Taxes, Duties, Imposts and Excises, to pay the Debts and provide for the common Defence and general Welfare of the United States; but all Duties, Imposts and Excises shall be uniform throughout the United States;

Here the original meaning of "welfare" should be addressed. The only other place the word appears in the Constitution is in the Preamble; in both places, it meant the general well-being of the citizenry as a whole, as in the wish "Fare the well". It did not mean paying the citizens with the citizen's own tax money, and it did not mean to establish taxes for charitable purposes, or to establish a federal "safety net" for unfortunates.

Constitutional "General Welfare" has been interpreted to be limited to the whole population's general well-being. "General Welfare" taxation and appropriation extend only to matters of national, as distinguished from local, welfare. Local well being is left to States, Counties and Townships as a simple matter of subsidiarity.

> "I cannot undertake to lay my finger on that article of the Constitution which granted a right to Congress of expending, on objects of benevolence, the money of their constituents."--*James Madison*

Believe it or not, the main source of government revenue during America's rise to economic power, before Income Tax existed, was *Tariff Taxes* on imported goods for sale in America. The only problem Congress wrestled with was keeping them low enough to not discourage imports altogether while using them to fund the whole government.

Since, first, the unconstitutional usurping of Constitutional authority and power by the Political Parties, and second, the Amendment XVI Income Tax, the major political contests fought between the two dominant Political Parties has been over taxing and spending for an ever growing list of citizen "welfare" benefits. Exactly what Tocqueville warned about:

— Bribing the voters with the citizen's own money.
— Training the citizenry in government dependency.

Today's Marxocrat Party thrives on citizen welfare, and today's Republicrat Party only argues over the ever growing quantity of it. No one truly opposes any of it. The Political Parties exist only for their own ever evolving political agendas, not for the Constitution.

Party and Campaign programs spend more time and money on poll-testing, focus-grouping, "scientific" and psychological evaluation of the voting public than they do on real matters of public importance. Politicians themselves have been reduced to being mere actors in the spotlight, driven and controlled by continually rewritten psychological scripts.

Political trickery rules the day. Professional Politicians today perform more as highly trained, practiced and polished Professional Actors, having memorized the latest poll-tested and focus-grouped psychologically convincing political scripts.

The contest itself is everything; the national interest is nothing.

# The Presidency and the Electoral College.

Article II of the Constitution describes the Presidency, his duties and how he is elected. When we go to the polls on the first Tuesday after the first Monday in November in every four-year National Election Cycle, we do not vote for President and Vice-President as such, but rather, for unnamed (on the ballot) *Electors*, who have been or are to be appointed by each Sovereign State in the USA.

The winning Electors will later elect the President and Vice-President.

> **Section. 1.** The executive Power shall be vested in a President of the United States of America. He shall hold his Office during the Term of four Years, and, together with the Vice President, chosen for the same Term, be elected, as follows:
>
> Each State shall appoint, in such Manner as the Legislature thereof may direct, a Number of Electors, equal to the whole Number of Senators and Representatives to which the State may be entitled in the Congress: but no Senator or Representative, or Person holding an Office of Trust or Profit under the United States, shall be appointed an Elector.

This Constitutional restricts Electors from being office holders, contenders for office or government employees. They will most typically be citizens who are dedicated and committed supporters of candidates for high office.

> The Congress may determine the Time of chusing the Electors, and the Day on which they shall give their Votes; which Day shall be the same throughout the United States.

The Electoral Election Process was given further order in Amendment XII, as follows:

> The Electors shall meet in their respective states, and vote by ballot for President and Vice-President, one of whom, at least, shall not be an inhabitant of the same state with themselves; they shall name in their ballots the person voted for as President, and in distinct ballots the person voted for as Vice-President, and they shall make distinct lists of all persons voted for as President, and of all persons voted for as Vice-President, and of the number of votes for each, which lists they shall sign and certify, and

15

transmit sealed to the seat of the government of the United States, directed to the President of the Senate; — The President of the Senate shall, in the presence of the Senate and House of Representatives, open all the certificates and the votes shall then be counted; — The person having the greatest number of votes for President, shall be the President, if such number be a majority of the whole number of Electors appointed; and if no person have such majority, then from the persons having the highest numbers not exceeding three on the list of those voted for as President, the House of Representatives shall choose immediately, by ballot, the President. But in choosing the President, the votes shall be taken by states, the representation from each state having one vote; a quorum for this purpose shall consist of a member or members from two-thirds of the states, and a majority of all the states shall be necessary to a choice. And if the House of Representatives shall not choose a President whenever the right of choice shall devolve upon them, before the fourth day of March next following, then the Vice-President shall act as President, as in the case of the death or other constitutional disability of the President. — The person having the greatest number of votes as Vice-President, shall be the Vice-President, if such number be a majority of the whole number of Electors appointed, and if no person have a majority, then from the two highest numbers on the list, the Senate shall choose the Vice-President; a quorum for the purpose shall consist of two-thirds of the whole number of Senators, and a majority of the whole number shall be necessary to a choice. But no person constitutionally ineligible to the office of President shall be eligible to that of Vice-President of the United States.

## Why Electors?  Why not Popular Vote?

The Electoral College, combined with the original Constitutional design of the Senate, ensures the sovereignty of each State within the USA.  It prevents highly populated States from overwhelming lower population States, and it prevents one or a few areas of America ruling all the rest of the entire country.  The Framers felt that the best way to build real national power was to distribute it rather than concentrate it.  The Senate (original design) and the Electoral College force the Federal Government to listen to the States.

If the Electoral College were to be eliminated, as constantly proposed by the Marxocrat Party, all national politics would take place only in the Liberal

Northeast and the Liberal West Coast. No Politician would ever even visit the rest of the nation, let alone campaign there. The politicians elected by the most populous cities would be making impractical laws and regulations for farmers, and for other things they know nothing about.

The States would eventually no longer be Sovereign States, but ruled by an all powerful Federal Government. State Legislators and Governors may as well go home and retire, for they will have nothing to do.

What is worse, now that the Congress is no longer the Congress of a Republic, but that of a Democracy, if we lose the Electoral College, the whole Republic will be transformed into a pure Democracy. A giant *Lynch Mob*. A Tyranny of the Majority. Doomed to fall into Socialism, which itself is doomed to economically fail, ultimately defaulting to the old time typical tyrannical government, the very thing that our original Constitution was designed to avoid.

> Democracy is the road to socialism. *--Karl Marx.*

> Democracy is indispensable to socialism. *--Vladimir Lenin.*

> The political form of a society wherein the proletariat is victorious in overthrowing the bourgeoisie will be a democratic republic. *--Vladimir Lenin.*

> [W]e must strengthen the United Nations as a first step toward a world government," …. "… We must change the basic structure of our global community … to a new system governed by a democratic UN federation. … Today the notion of unlimited national sovereignty means international anarchy. We must replace the anarchic law of force with a civilized force of law. *--Walter Cronkite.*

## What does the President do?

As far as what pertains to us, the free citizenry, he acts as the Chief Executive Officer of the USA. His primary duty, therefore, is to execute law, as per Section 3 of Article II:

> "… he shall take Care that the Laws be faithfully executed …"

Comrade President Obama (peace be upon him) demonstrates more than any of his predecessors a willingness and an unresisted ability to enforce only laws of his choosing, and "laws" not even in existence, and to ignore and even violate existing legitimate legislated laws that are not in his favor. He behaves precisely as a dictator.

He unconstitutionally uses Executive Orders (and so-called "Actions") having nothing to do with emergency national defense or security emergencies to just put into place personal agenda items, all of which seem to be harmful to America and to national security in some way.

Just look at his hand picked "Czars" and cout the anti-Americans, the Seditionists and Communists among them.

Just look at his hand-picked National Security Advisors and count the *Moslem Brotherhood* anti-American, Civilization Jihadist-Terrorists among them.

He illegally holds open our borders, encourages border violation and virtual invasion by foreigners, and *purposely does not enforce* existing immigration laws, and when States try to protect their citizenry from all the criminal aliens entering their States, he has his Attorney General sue them, for trying to enforce existing law themselves, for the protection of their own citizenry.

He consistently and continually promotes anti-white racism, anti-American and anti-Western sentiment. He encourages and gives aid and comfort to Soros-funded and other Globalist-funded, and Marxocrat-funded, Alinskyite-organized, violent, racist anti-police organizations, while ordering his Attorney General to interfere as much as possible with the local police in areas targeted for sedition, revolution and riots, under the false title of "rallies" or "demonstrations".

He issues "edicts" from on high protecting the *imagined-into-being "rights"* of twisted perverts to enter and remain in opposite sex public rest rooms, and other such dangerous, stupid and infuriating "policies".

He blatantly and quite obviously promotes social chaos and disorder.

The exact opposite of the words in the Preamble of the Constitution, to:

> "form a more perfect Union, establish Justice, insure domestic Tranquility, provide for the common defence, promote the general Welfare, and secure the Blessings of Liberty to ourselves and our Posterity".

And he gets away with it, with the full support of our now totally *Culturally Marxist* News Media and Upper Academia. And with no resistance from the Republicrat Party, other than harmless bloviating.

The "Establishment" Republicrat Party is obviously in cahoots with the Marxocrat Party.

Establishment Republicrats are either *Politically Corrected* and intimidated into impotence and incompetence, or they, too, are now *Culturally Marxified* enemies of America. And also enemies of Christians, white people, local police, heterosexuals, normal people and *Western Civilization*, just like all leading Academics, leading Journalists and popular comedians.

## The Supreme Court.

Article III describes the Supreme Court and its duties. The first paragraph:

> **Section. 1.** The judicial Power of the United States shall be vested in one supreme Court, and in such inferior Courts as the Congress may from time to time ordain and establish. The Judges, both of the supreme and inferior Courts, shall hold their Offices during good Behaviour, and shall, at stated Times, receive for their Services a Compensation, which shall not be diminished during their Continuance in Office.

It seems to me that no one has ever paid any attention whatsoever to the clause "shall hold their Offices during good behaviour". Never in the entire history of the USA has any Justice been removed for "bad behaviour", although we have seen Justices (like Senators, like Representatives, like Presidents) *directly violate* the very Constitution they all solemnly swore to uphold in their very oaths of office.

*Many times.*

And nothing happens.

The jurisdiction of the Supreme Court (as far as you and I are concerned) is limited to the Constitution itself and to legislated federal law. Issues outside of Article I Section 8 are not legitimately subject to being addressed by the Supreme Court (or by the Congress, or by the President).

But they most typically address everything that comes their way when a ruling could possibly support the current Marxocrat Party political agenda item of the moment.

- Then, they will unconstitutionally hear cases that are clearly out of scope and outside federal government authority, clearly matters for States and lower jurisdictions to properly handle.
- Then, they will unconstitutionally violate the principle of the Separation Of Powers and "legislate from the bench", making new law by way of establishing case law *legal precedent*. From that moment on, the "new law" will be held to be "Constitutional", and an actual law, despite never having been legislated, per Article I of the Constitution.

Some of the worst examples:

1. 1947 Everson case (Separation of Church and State)
2. Roe v Wade and Doe v Bolton
3. Obamacare
4. Homosexual "Marriage"

There are more; these are to me the most egregious. The effects of these decisions is to work to weaken if not destroy Christian faith in the citizenry, to weaken if not destroy any sense of Christian morality, to grow the government enormously, and to override and overpower existing Constitutional rights with new, *conjured-into-being* minority rights of the the supposedly aggrieved minorities.

The Court increasingly and now consistently acts in direct opposition to the very purpose of the American Constitutional Government, which is to protect the Natural Law Rights of the Citizenry to Equality, Life, Liberty and Property, and *to protect them from the government itself*. These are the rights of the Declaration itself, and they are all specifically defined *Constitutional Rights* as well. Yet today, in the Court's opinion, non-existent homosexual "rights" override existing Constitutional Rights, just as one example among the many.

## The Constitutional Rights.

In the website treatment of going back to a *No Party America* we laid out the Constitutional Rights of the American Citizenry, as follows:

- To not be deprived of Equality, Life, Liberty or Property without conviction of criminal offense under due process of just law.
- To move freely.

- To assemble peaceably.

- To keep and bear arms.

- To assemble in an independent well-disciplined militia.

- To communicate with the world.

- To express or publish one's opinions or those of others.

- To practice one's religion.

- To be secure in one's person, house, papers, vehicle, and effects against unreasonable searches and seizures.

- To enjoy privacy in all matters in which the rights of others are not violated.

- To acquire, have and use the means necessary to exercise the above natural rights and pursue happiness, specifically including:

  1. A private residence from which others may be excluded.
  2. Tools needed for one's livelihood.
  3. Personal property which others may be denied the use of.
  4. Arms suitable for personal and community defense.

- To enter into contracts, and thereby acquire contractual rights, to secure the means to exercise the above natural rights.
- To enjoy equally the rights, privileges and protections of personhood as established by law.
- To petition an official for redress of grievances and get action thereon in accordance with law, subject to the resources available thereto.

- To petition a legislator and get consideration thereof, subject to resources available thereto.
- To petition a court for redress of grievances and get a decision thereon, subject to resources available thereto.
- Not to have one's natural rights individually disabled except through due process of law, which includes:

In criminal cases:

1. Not to be charged for a major crime but by indictment by a Grand Jury, except while serving in the military, or while serving in the Militia during time of war or public danger.
2. Not to be charged more than once for the same offense.
3. Not to be compelled to testify against oneself.
4. Not to have excessive bail required.
5. To be tried by an impartial jury from the state and district in which the events took place.
6. To have a jury of at least six for a misdemeanor, and at least twelve for a felony.
7. To a speedy trial.
8. To a public trial.
9. To have the assistance of counsel of one's choice.
10. To be informed of the nature and cause of the accusation.
11. To be confronted with the witnesses against one.
12. To have compulsory process for obtaining favorable witnesses.
13. To have each charge proved beyond a reasonable doubt.
14. To have a verdict by a unanimous vote of the jury, which shall not be held to account for its verdict.
15. To have the jury decide on both the facts of the case and the constitutionality, jurisdiction, and applicability of the law.
16. Upon conviction, to have each disablement separately and explicitly proven as justified and necessary based on the facts and verdict.
17. To have a sentence which explicitly states all disablements, and is final in that once rendered no further disablements may be imposed for the same offense.
18. Not to have a cruel or unusual punishment inflicted upon oneself.

In civil cases:

1. To trial by an impartial jury from the state and district in which the events took place where the issue in question is either a natural right or property worth more than $20.

2. In taking of one's property for public use, to be given just compensation therefor.
3. To have compulsory process for obtaining favorable witnesses.

In all cases:

1. To have process only upon legal persons able to defend themselves, either natural persons or corporate persons that are represented by a natural person as agent, and who are present, competent, and duly notified, except, in cases of disappearance or abandonment, after public notice and a reasonable period of time.
2. Not to be ordered to give testimony or produce evidence beyond what is necessary to the proper conduct of the process.
3. To enjoy equally the rights and privileges of citizenship as established by law.
4. To vote in elections that are conducted fairly and honestly, by secret ballot.
5. To exercise general police powers to defend the community and enforce the laws, subject to legal orders of higher-ranking officials.
6. To receive militia training.

Anyone anywhere on earth who reads these rights will recognize the unique nature of the USA. The American Government was instituted specifically to protect these citizen rights *from itself*. It is the bound, sworn duty of the President to proactively defend these rights of the citizens. It is the bound, sworn duty of the Congress to not infringe them in any way with conflicting law. It is the bound, sworn duty of the Court to hold them superior to any other "rights" found anywhere other than in the Constitution.

This is just black and white, simple common sense law.

## The States.

The problem the Framers wrestled with was how to keep the several Sovereign States actually *Sovereign Entities* while subjecting them, or rather having them subject themselves, to a *National Constitution*. A Constitution handling foreign affairs and diplomacy, national military forces, border integrity and immigration policy, etc., and, perhaps most importantly, recognizing State Citizen's absolute Rights under the National Constitution.

Sovereign State Governments were not to be free to violate the Constitutional Rights of State Citizens. And, citizens were to be free to move and relocate between States, as they pleased.

It took a lot of haggling and compromising to get it done.

The whole of the Constitution could not be ratified by the States without inclusion of the Bill Of Rights - the First Ten Amendments - enshrining in fixed, supreme national law the the rights of the people and the rights of the States. Americans are all aware (or they should be aware) of the citizen rights established in the Bill Of Rights; it used to be that any student in any school, by about the fourth or fifth grade, could recite them. Today, most citizens are still at least vaguely familiar with the First and Second Amendments.

## Bill Of Rights

### Amendment I

Congress shall make no law respecting an establishment of religion, or prohibiting the free exercise thereof; or abridging the freedom of speech, or of the press; or the right of the people peaceably to assemble, and to petition the Government for a redress of grievances.

### Amendment II

A well regulated Militia, being necessary to the security of a free State, the right of the people to keep and bear Arms, shall not be infringed.

### Amendment III

No Soldier shall, in time of peace be quartered in any house, without the consent of the Owner, nor in time of war, but in a manner to be prescribed by law.

### Amendment IV

The right of the people to be secure in their persons, houses, papers, and effects, against unreasonable searches and seizures, shall not be violated, and no Warrants shall issue, but upon probable cause, supported by Oath or affirmation, and particularly describing the place to be searched, and the persons or things to be seized.

## Amendment V

No person shall be held to answer for a capital, or otherwise infamous crime, unless on a presentment or indictment of a Grand Jury, except in cases arising in the land or naval forces, or in the Militia, when in actual service in time of War or public danger; nor shall any person be subject for the same offence to be twice put in jeopardy of life or limb; nor shall be compelled in any criminal case to be a witness against himself, nor be deprived of life, liberty, or property, without due process of law; nor shall private property be taken for public use, without just compensation.

## Amendment VI

In all criminal prosecutions, the accused shall enjoy the right to a speedy and public trial, by an impartial jury of the State and district wherein the crime shall have been committed, which district shall have been previously ascertained by law, and to be informed of the nature and cause of the accusation; to be confronted with the witnesses against him; to have compulsory process for obtaining witnesses in his favor, and to have the Assistance of Counsel for his defence.

## Amendment VII

In Suits at common law, where the value in controversy shall exceed twenty dollars, the right of trial by jury shall be preserved, and no fact tried by a jury, shall be otherwise re-examined in any Court of the United States, than according to the rules of the common law.

## Amendment VIII

Excessive bail shall not be required, nor excessive fines imposed, nor cruel and unusual punishments inflicted.

## Amendment IX

The enumeration in the Constitution, of certain rights, shall not be construed to deny or disparage others retained by the people.

## Amendment X

The powers not delegated to the United States by the Constitution, nor prohibited by it to the States, are reserved to the States respectively, or to the people.

The Ninth and Tenth Amendments are of vital importance to the ingenuous original design of the Constitution. Combined with the original design of the Senate to be a body of Statesmen rather than Politicians for legislation of new law, and with the original design of the Electoral College for the election of Presidents, they make national elections into *Geographic* Elections, rather than simple Democratic *Popular* national elections. They give States a significant voice in the process.

Not only are State governments and the citizens thereof free to recognize rights outside of (and not conflicting with) Constitutional Rights, but they are free to legislate State law any way they want to, so long as it does not violate Constitutional Law. If it is outside of Article I Section 8, the States have free reign over it, and the Federal Government has nothing whatsoever to say about it.

(Unless they violate the Constitution, which they are currently doing.)

Furthermore, some unheard of County in Kansas, or some small town in that County, can actually have a measurable affect on the outcome of a National Election, rather than having been smothered by the votes from some one or two populous areas of the whole nation.

Now that the Senate has been made "Democratic", if you take the Electoral College out of the picture, then heavily populated New York and/or California will rule *all of America*, and the States will have no voice and play no part in the national political process.

## **Christian Morality of the American Citizenry.**

The reason that the new nation in America rocketed to such incredible economic power was what drew Alexis de Tocqueville to come to America and research. And what he found was what the Framers already knew; that the new American Republic would only properly function with a predominantly highly moral citizenry. They were right. America was great because here people were a "good" people. When the people ceased being good, the nation would go into decline. The American Republic, as designed, was totally dependent upon a good and decent citizenry.

"Our Constitution was made only for a moral and religious people. It is wholly inadequate to the government of any other." –*John Adams.*

"It can not be emphasized too strongly or too often that this great nation of ours was founded, not by religionists, but by Christians ... not on religions, but on the gospel of Jesus Christ." –*Patrick Henry.*

"Only a virtuous people are capable of freedom. As nations become corrupt and vicious, they have more need of masters." –*Benjamin Franklin.*

"The sum of all is, if we would most truly enjoy the gift of Heaven, let us become a virtuous people; then shall we both deserve and enjoy it. While, on the other hand, if we are universally vicious and debauched in our manners, though the form of our Constitution carries the *face* of the most exalted freedom, we shall in reality be the most abject slaves." –*Samuel Adams.*

"Of all the dispositions and habits which lead to political prosperity, religion and morality are indispensable supports. In vain would that man claim the tribute of patriotism who should labor to subvert these great pillars of human happiness, these firmest props of the duties of men and citizens ... Let it simply be asked, where is the security for property, for reputation, for life, if the sense of religious obligation desert the oaths which are the instruments of investigation in courts of justice?" –*George Washington.*

"Without God there is no virtue because there is no prompting of the conscience ... without God there is a coarsening of the society; without God democracy will not and cannot long endure ... If we ever forget that we are One Nation Under God, then we will be a Nation gone under." –*Ronald Reagan.*

"The link between culture and faith is not only necessary for culture but also for faith. A faith that does not become culture is a faith not fully embraced, not fully appreciated and not faithfully lived." –*John Paul the Great.*

And yet, for *centuries* now, we have increasingly been tricked into "keeping our religion to ourselves" as if it were something that needed to be hidden. Our Christian religion is the very source of our moral goodness, and we have been psychologically tricked into "compartmentalizing" it and keeping it out of public discourse. We are socially encouraged to "put our religion aside" in social circumstances, and we increasingly do that, despite the simple fact that,

> *Putting our religion aside, ever, is strictly against our religion.*

Christian religion is not something to do, but something to live. And if we do not live out our faith, we will lose it. No one can be a part-time Christian, and Christian Morality is not a part-time subject, capable of being put aside in any particular circumstances. It touches everything we say and write and do. When it does not, then we are no longer true Christians.

While there is no real gain to be made in arguing specific Catholic or Protestant theological points in the political arena, there is indeed much to be gained or lost in arguing specific Catholic and/or Protestant moral points in the political arena. On moral points of order affecting political subjects under contest, Catholic and Protestant Bibles are in full accord. A thing is either moral, or it is not moral.

Judaeo-Christian Morality is and has been from the beginning the unique American sense of right versus wrong, and there is no other such civilized and civilizing moral order in existence. When we lose this common national sense of morality we will lose the whole nation.

## Religious Plurality, Anti-Institution sentiment and Disestablishment.

In Post Reformation Europe, as state-enforced religion became more and more unmanageable, an informal religious pluralism arose. People who opposed the state religion in most states became so numerous that they couldn't be controlled without massive violence, and Europe was exhausted by decades of the violence of the Reformation Wars and no one wanted any more of it, including Kings and Parliaments.

Vast numbers of state citizens not of the state religion needed such things as,

- either admittance to and membership in the state church, or release from paying tithes to it;
- a voice in government in states that allowed votes, but only by those holding the state religion.

And people wanted these things even though they did not want to fully practice the state religion. And the numbers just kept growing. In some states tithes were taken out of taxes, and growing segments of the population resented that. In many states, non-state churches were actually built and attended and tithed, illegally, but allowed to persist by state governments just tired of the years of bloodshed.

Giving birth to and accelerating the popular anti-institution sentiment was, of course, the bloody French Revolution, which sought to outlaw religion and clericalism altogether. They beheaded as many priests, monks and nuns as they did nobles and aristocrats. It failed, of course, to destroy faith in God; they only drove it underground, and added Militant Secularism into the growing "Pluralistic Mix". Eventually, France, too, would come to allow various churches to exist and operate, so long as the disciples kept their religion to themselves and off the streets.

The predominant compromise came to be that state churches would allow non-members entry, provided they were Baptized Christians. They would be "imperfect" tithing members, who would hopefully be evangelized fully into the flock through regular church attendance.

At the same time, non-state Christian religions were more or less officially allowed to establish themselves in the state.

This was Christian "Pluralism".

Something similar happened in the American Colonies. As the roaring economy of America drew more and more immigrants from Europe, it soon came to pass that the immigrant population of various Christian faiths outnumbered the Colonial citizenry holding the Colonial faith. Among them were Baptists and Methodists who fiercely defended "Freedom Of Conscience" and refused to pay tithes to official Colonial churches, and who were very public about their grievance that they had no voice in government, simply because of their faith, and despite their numbers.

And so, as in Europe, Colonial churches began admitting Baptized Christians of other denomination into their membership, as "imperfect" members, to be evangelized into full communion. After all, they were all Christians. Also, as in Europe, non-Colonial churches were allowed to be built, tithed and attended, at first very exceptionally here and there, but before too long these new churches were all over the place.

The Disestablishment movement began to dismantle the idea of State churches in Europe and Colonial churches in America. But "Religious Pluralism" had an unpleasant and unforeseen consequence. Pluralism in congregations also began to disestablish actual original churches, as membership fell and all the outside churches grew. The hoped for evangelization of the imperfect members was working in reverse. Established members were being evangelized by the imperfect members, rather than the other way round.

## Anti-Catholicism brings on Anti-Institutionalism.

As the Protestant institutional churches were dwindling in membership, more and more Catholic immigrants were coming into America, and not necessarily to Catholic Maryland. They were all over the place. It became a crisis (in the Protestant view) with the Irish Potato Famine, when they began to come in the millions, bringing their Catholicism with them, and building churches everywhere.

Unlike the denominations, the Catholic Church was still a very strong, very visible, very unchanged *Institutional Church*, not being "Pluralized" out of being by its own membership. (Yet.) American Protestantism, *universally*, saw this as a national crisis, because, as they were assured by their own Protestant upbringing, the Catholic Church was an Institution that intended to dominate all, and rule the world. They saw Catholicism as an actual *menace*. If there was one thing all the denominations could agree and unite on, it was anti-Catholicism.

The rock solid *Institution* of Catholicism scared the hell out of them.

It was this fear, I believe, that began the general anti-institution sentiment that would grow and grow, and that would eventually be capitalized on by evil Marxism. If you look at the closing lines of the Manifesto, you will see that Marxism seeks the "revolutionary" destruction of all existing *institutions*. It is a "revolutionary movement against the existing social and political order of things." It calls for "the forcible overthrow of all existing social conditions."

That threat is aimed at the Catholic Church just as much as it is aimed at the USA. And at Protestantism.

On its own, the anti-institution sentiment grew among the denominations to the point that institutional Protestant churches began to be denied by denominations, and new denominations sprang up denying denominationalism, and denying that they themselves were denominations. "Non-denominational" denominations came into being. (I submit that if they hold to Luther's established dogmas of Sola Scriptura and Sola Fide, then they are denominations descended from Luther's Protestantism, whatever else they may choose to call themselves.)

Out of all of this *Freedom Of Conscience, Religious Pluralism, Disestablishment* and *Anti-Institution* sentiment arose the super-individualistic, *One Man Church* heresy. The idea that I can be my own church. That "Church" is not an institution, or a worldly thing, but a system of religious beliefs. In this holding, the one-man-church doesn't need any building or any institution or any liturgy, or anything at all to do with any organized church. All he needs is his Bible and himself. Despite what the Bible says about that, many believe it.

## Marxism multiplies and capitalizes on Pluralistic Multiculturalism.

As we said in *Anti-God, Anti-Nature and Anti-USA*, Marx wrote his manifesto in direct reaction to the new "Classless Society" established by the American Constitutional Republic. He hated the idea that someone had beaten Communism to the punch in successfully eliminating classes and nobility and all-powerful government. As we said there:

> I submit that Karl Marx developed Marxism, circa 1848, as a direct reaction to and as a counter-ideology of, the meteoric economic rise of the USA.

Marxism, by its own definition, is a mortal enemy of religion and of the liberty of man. But Marxism, like Satan, takes on many, many different disguises and appearances.

That the re-distributive, collective and communal "Social Perfecting" ideologies of Marxism have come to dominate education, academia, journalism, entertainment and even politics in America, and even *religion* in America, is a clear, obvious and easily verifiable fact.

31

Despite their falseness, and despite the underlying evil and socially destructive intent of Marxism, its successful psychological projection of itself as "good" for society has recruited believing disciples in all walks of life.

*We The People* allowed it to get on the *Political Bus* with us, and it has easily and "diplomatically" maneuvered itself into the *driver's seat.*

Marx himself preferred Marxism to come to power through direct bloody Revolution. When all the Revolutions beginning in 1848 all ultimately failed all over Europe, Marxism changed to foment "Progressive" social change leading to eventual Revolution, while still inciting violent Revolutions here and there, wherever it seemed possible.

It is "Progressive" Marxism that has come to the verge of dominating the whole world, or throwing it into the levels of utter chaos and disorder necessary for an opportune faux *Revolution* to fix it all.

Just look at the *European Union* as an example, and ask yourself how such an obviously stupid organization could have even come to exist, without the Progressive prodding of Marxism toward Globalism and out of all sense of national sovereignty and national self-interest. The European Union *epitomizes* the destructive intent of the "Diversity" and "Multicultural" socially destructive movements of Marxism.

People have been taught to believe that diversity is good, and not bad.

Just as demonized *Human Institutions* are seen as bad and not good.

Marxism seeks to turn us all into a bland, unidentifiable social mixture. Despite the fact that virtue and vice are absolutely incompatible. Few see that all this is being done with an actual evil purpose behind it.

Attempts at instigating violent revolution in America, such as during the 1960s campus burnings and race riots, failed only in part; they also succeeded in part. They brought down an American Presidency, and lost a war against Communism in Vietnam through violence in the streets incited by false news reporting, and they promoted promiscuity and sexual licentiousness through a successful *Sexual Revolution.* All good "steps" toward the long-term Marxist goals.

But Marxism made (and continues to make) good progress through programs of increasing Social Justice and Multiculturalism. People today actually believe these things are somehow *good* for society. In a nation devoid of social classes, Marxists invented new classes, and set them against each other, through a *Divide And Conquer* program building up "Grievance Classes" alienated from the larger nation. All aimed at stirring up eventual *Class Warfare*.

Whatever cannot be achieved by violent Revolutionary actions is achieved slowly and steadily, step by step, through Political Progressivism combined with grass-roots Alsinskyism, Cloward-Piven Welfare-overloading and a continuous steady diet of anti-American pro-Communist Propaganda disguised as News.

The chief strategists at the top of the Marxist plan of American destruction, exemplified by the Obamas and the Clintons, are ungodly men, pointing the finger of ungodliness at the most godly among us. True racists pointing the finger of racism at the non-racists; true sexists, pointing the finger of sexism at the non-sexists; true bigots, pointing the finger of bigotry at the non-bigots.

They are all that they falsely accuse their opposition of being.

They can't get race, sex, "gender", etc., etc., etc., off of their bigoted and anti-American tiny little Marxist minds.

They blatantly oppose Truth. They obviously oppose God, Nature and even Scientific, Empirical *Reality*. They clearly and openly oppose what we are supposed to stand for: Equality, Life, Liberty, the Pursuit of Happiness and Private Property.

(They oppose it for us, of course; not for themselves.)

They oppose *God*; they are *ungodly*.

## **Only a return to Christian Morality will save Constitutional America.**

Pray that President Elect Donald Trump comes to recognize that fact.

What ever human imperfections he may have, and whatever else he may be, he is no Marxist. He is a "real" man, i.e., he lives a very practical life in the real world, and he deals with real-world problems in a real-world way, largely unaffected by political ideologies. If there is one thing he is not, it is any kind of polished politician. His first love, I have come to believe, is America herself, and her people.

He intends to restore her to her former greatness.

But America's former greatness was based on her ingenuous original Constitutional design, in which the People were freed by their own government, with protected Natural Law Rights, to just go ahead and *govern themselves*, and seek their own better self interest.

The fly in that ointment is that, before a people can be self-governing, they must first be highly moral. Before a whole people can be moral, *individual citizens* must be moral, in their overwhelming majority.

Cultural Marxism, and in particular Gramsci Marxism, continue to *demoralize* the American people, and turn them away from God, and from Nature, and even from America's best interest. Immorality will bring us down before any foreign enemy.

Many citizens today equate "freedom" with sexual license. But sexual license, like any form of sin, is not freeing but enslaving. It is addictive. All sin is addictive. Man cannot be truly free until and unless he is free of the temptations of the world, and that can only come from a turning to God, to cooperating with His saving Grace, and obeying His law.

It's a kind of freedom Marxism cannot understand, and cannot achieve.

To have a self-governing nation requires a self-governing people, and that means a predominant majority of self-governing individuals. You cannot be self governing if you believe that "anything goes". If you cannot control yourself, you will need to be controlled. If a whole people cannot control itself, it will need to be controlled. That's what Marxism aims at: *Making you uncontrollable.*

Resist the enemy. Resist temptation. Turn your face to God. *Turn from sin.* You don't need it, and America doesn't need it.

> If my people who are called by my name humble themselves, and pray and seek my face, and turn from their wicked ways, then I will hear from heaven, and will forgive their sin and heal their land.--*2 Chron 7:14*

# ABOUT THE AUTHOR

I am nobody you ever heard of. This little booklet is one webpage out of my website, which is http://www.catholicamericanthinker.com/. Discussions with people who are not "on-line" convinced me of a need to get some of my website information out in printed form for those who are interested but not computer savvy. To me, religion and politics are vitally important topics, which are erroneously verboten in public discourse.

Entirely too many American citizens today simply do not know, for instance, how US Senators were intended to be appointed by State Governments, and not be elected politicians like the members of the House. Or, the purpose and critical importance of the Electoral College.

Every American should know these things.

So, I'm making this as cheep as I can make it, just to make it available. If you have relatives or friends who don't get on-line and who need to know about American politics and American religion, *pass it on*.

For more in depth information, see my book,
Culture = Relligion + Politics

God bless.

www.ingramcontent.com/pod-product-compliance
Lightning Source LLC
Chambersburg PA
CBHW070241290526
45789CB00004B/1713